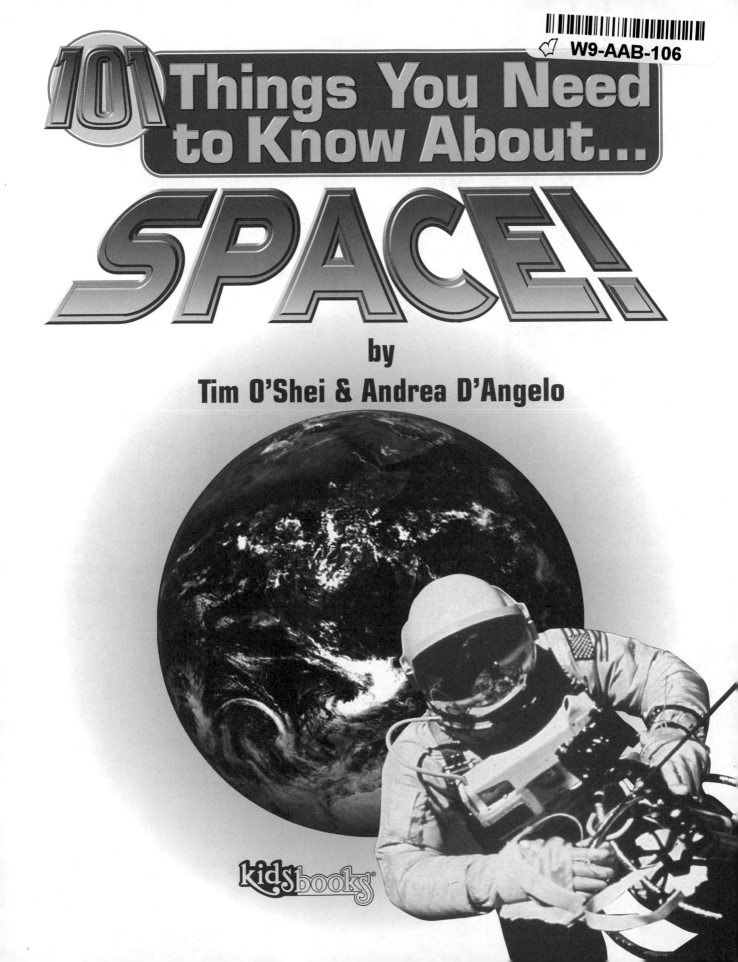

101 Things You Need to Know About... SPACE!

by

Tim O'Shei & Andrea D'Angelo

kidsbooks

The authors thank astronauts Barbara Morgan and Jeff Ashby for their research assistance.

Photo Credits

AP/Wide World: pp. 13, 22-23, 24-25, 28, 30 (both), 32 (both), 33 (all), 34 (bottom), 39 (bottom), 41 (right)

Howard S. Friedman: pp. 10-11

The Granger Collection: p. 8

NASA: pp. 4-5, 6-7, 12 (bottom), 26, 31

NASA Ames Research Center: pp. 44-45, 47

NASA Goddard Space Flight Center: pp. 14, 16

NASA Headquarters—Greatest Images of NASA: cover, pp. 2 (top), 3, 20, 25 (top right), 34 (top), 35, 37, 40, 48

NASA Jet Propulsion Laboratory: pp. 14-15, 17, 18-19, 21, 27

NASA Johnson Space Center: pp. 25 (center), 38, 39 (top), 41 (left)

NASA Kennedy Space Center: pp. 29 (left & bottom right), 43 (bottom)

NASA Marshall Space Flight Center: pp. 25 (top & bottom), 36, 42, 43 (top)

Carol Russo Design: pp. 9, 12 (top)

Visit us at **www.kidsbooks.com**

Welcome to the Universe!

Do you gaze at the night sky and dream about flying to the stars? Have you ever watched a space shuttle roar off its launch pad and soar into the sky? Do you sometimes wonder if living beings are lurking in a corner of the universe that we haven't yet discovered?

The following pages will fuel your imagination about all those things and more. You will find out how space shuttles work. You will discover what scientists are doing to find life on other planets. You also will soon realize why flying to the stars could be a very long trip!

Along the way, you will be introduced to machines, people, and even animals that have flown into space. You will meet some real astronauts, learn how they train, and even find out why M&Ms are a real mess up in space!

For just a little while, take your eyes off the sky and aim them at these pages. After reading this book, you will be a smarter stargazer.

Outer space awaits, so let's take a ride!

Space Talk

What is space?

1. Space—also called outer space—is everything outside Earth's atmosphere. *Space* is the key word, because it is mostly empty space! If you could travel into space in any direction, anytime, and for as long as you wanted, you could go for many years without hitting anything.

Up, up in the atmosphere

2. An *atmosphere* is the layer of gases that surround a planet. The gases are held in place by the planet's gravity. Unlike other planets, Earth's atmosphere includes lots of oxygen, which is what allows animal life—including us humans—to exist here.

We are closer than you think!

3. Outer space is very close to Earth—only 50 to 70 miles away from Earth's surface. How close is that? A car can drive that distance in less than an hour. NASA astronaut Jeff Ashby describes it another way: "If Earth was a basketball," he says, "space would be only one sixteenth of an inch above it."

It is pretty big out there!

Our planet is a tiny, tiny part of what is out there. Here is how it breaks down:

4. Earth is one of nine planets in our solar system. A *solar system* is a group of planets that revolve around a star. *(For more on our solar system, see pages 10-11.)*

5. Our solar system is part of a galaxy called the Milky Way. A *galaxy* is a group of stars, planets, and other related bodies (everything from space dust to moons). Our galaxy seems huge to us, but it is quite small as galaxies go. A large galaxy can include hundreds of billions—yes, *billions*—of stars. There are many galaxies in the universe. We can't see them all, so we can't say exactly how many. Scientists used to estimate that there are about 10 billion galaxies. Now, with higher-tech tools, such as the Hubble Space Telescope, the estimate is 50 billion galaxies—or more.

6. The universe—also known as the cosmos—is simply everything—all that is out there.

planet Earth

Meet Our Star

How old are you now?

7. The star at the center of our solar system is the sun. Compared to Earth, it is huge (about 109 times as large as Earth). Compared to other stars, though, it is medium-sized. Most stars of similar size last for 10 billion years. Our sun is middle-aged—about 4.6 billion years old.

the sun

Good day, sunshine!

8. The sun is our solar system's hot spot. It is about 11,000 degrees Fahrenheit at the surface! It is so hot at the surface that there *isn't* a real surface. It is way too hot for anything solid or liquid to exist. The sun is made mostly of two gases, hydrogen and helium. Its great heat comes from nuclear reactions taking place in its core.

Going in circles

9. Our solar system is like one big merry-go-round. At the center is the sun. Around it spin the nine planets, each in its own oval path. Those paths are called *orbits.* Some planets have objects orbiting them, too. For instance, our moon orbits Earth while Earth is orbiting the sun.

At the center of things

10. Up until about 500 years ago, people generally believed that Earth was the center of the universe. They thought that the sun, the moon, the other planets, and all the stars revolved around Earth. A Polish astronomer named Nicolaus Copernicus *(NIK-uh-LAY-us koh-PUR-nih-kus),* who lived from 1473 to 1547, said otherwise. (An *astronomer* is a scientist who studies objects in space.) By studying old astronomy charts, Copernicus noticed that the planets did not always seem to travel in the same direction. The reason, he realized, is that Earth is moving, too!

Hot debate

11. Copernicus claimed that Earth and all the other planets orbit the sun. Earth, he said, takes a year to make one orbit of the sun. He also said that Earth spins on its axis as it moves through space. (What is an axis? Imagine a pole going straight down the middle of a ball, with the ball spinning around it.) Many people refused to accept Copernicus's ideas, which fueled hot debate for the next 300 years.

Galileo

Proving Copernicus right

12. In 1609, an Italian astronomer named Galileo Galilei *(ga-luh-LEE-oh ga-lih-LAY)* did something that Copernicus could not—he used a telescope to study the sky. Galileo noticed moons near Jupiter, and saw that they were revolving around the huge planet. This was proof of Copernicus's theory. Even then, many people did not believe it. It took a couple of centuries before people generally agreed with Copernicus and Galileo. Earth does indeed revolve around the sun.

Day vs. night

13. A day on any planet is the length of time it takes that planet to make one complete turn on its axis. In one day, we see the sun rise, then set, then rise again to the same position in the sky. The faster a planet rotates, the shorter its day.

14. On Earth, one turn takes 24 hours. On Jupiter, a day lasts only 10 hours.

15. A Mars day is about a half an hour longer than an Earth day.

16. A day on Mercury is more than 1,400 hours long! That is about 59 Earth days.

Hey, where did it go?

17. An *eclipse* is when one body in space blocks our view of
another. (This happens now and then because of all those orbits
taking place.) In a *solar eclipse (see picture below)*, the moon
lines up between the sun and Earth, blocking our view of the
sun. In a *lunar eclipse (see picture below)*, Earth lines up
between the sun and the moon, blocking the sun's light. As
Earth's shadow falls on the moon, the moon seems to disappear.

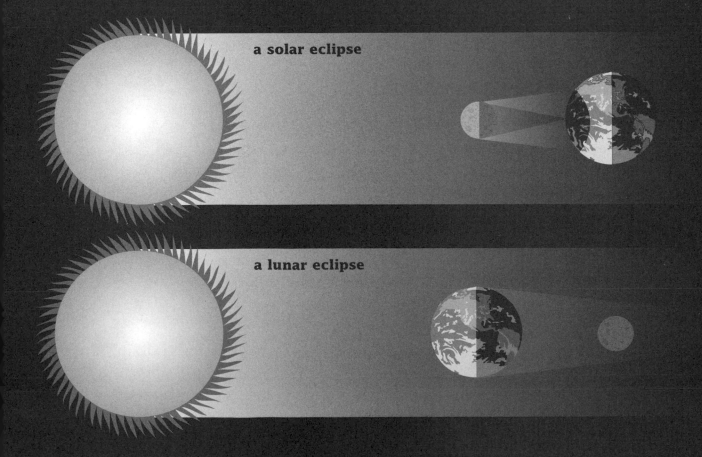

a solar eclipse

a lunar eclipse

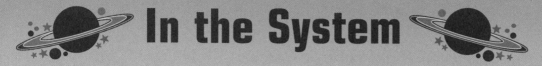

In the System

The lineup of nine

18. The nine planets in our solar system, starting with the one closest to the sun, are Mercury, Venus, Earth, Mars, Jupiter, Saturn, Uranus, Neptune, and Pluto. Want an easy way to remember them, in order? The first letter of each word in this sentence matches each planet's first letter: **M**y **V**ery **E**ducated **M**other **J**ust **S**howed **U**s **N**ine **P**lanets.

Pluto

Neptune

Mercury

Sun

Venus

Jupiter

Earth

19. The four planets closest to the sun—Mercury, Venus, Earth, and Mars—are known as the rocky planets, for a good reason. They are made of rock.

20. Four of the five outer planets are made mostly of gas. The exception is Pluto, which is made of rock. It is covered in water, ice, and frozen methane. That is one cold planet!

our solar system

Mars

Saturn

Uranus

Fellow travelers

21. Pieces of rock that orbit the sun are called *asteroids*. Asteroids are too small to be considered planets, although some astronomers call them *minor planets* or *planetoids*.

Nice belt!

22. More than half a million of those rock chunks orbit our sun in a ring known as the *asteroid belt*. The asteroid belt is located between Mars and Jupiter. (You can see it in this picture.)

A tenth planet?

23. What is nearly as red as Mars, smaller than Pluto, and considers a temperature of –400 degrees Fahrenheit to be a hot day? The answer is Sedna, a faraway object discovered in early 2004. Some astronomers think that it may be the tenth planet in our solar system. Others think that it may be a large cloud of icy objects, some of which break free and become comets. *(For more on comets, see pages 14-15.)* Astronomers can't yet get a good enough look to tell for sure. Sedna is *way* out there: eight billion miles from Earth. (That is three times as far as Pluto!)

New

First Quarter

Full

Last Quarter

Many Moons

Rock 'n' rotate

24. Moons are natural *satellites*—objects that orbit a planet or other large body in space. Many moons, such as Earth's, are made of rock. (One of Saturn's moons is more than half ice.) There are more than 100 moons in our solar system. The only planets in our solar system without a moon are Mercury and Venus.

Our moon

25. Earth's moon is one fourth the size of Earth.

26. If you watch Earth's moon every night for 27 days, it will seem to change shape. It gradually goes through four main steps called *phases*: **new moon, first-quarter moon, full moon,** and **last-quarter moon.** *(See the chart at left.)* Then the cycle starts all over again. Between a new moon and first-quarter moon, we see a crescent that grows a little larger every day. Between a full and last-quarter moon, the crescent gradually grows smaller.

Moonlight is fake!

27. Moonlight is a big part of our lives. It helps us see at night, adds spookiness to scary stories, and casts a lovely glow over warm summer evenings. But true moonlight does not exist. The moon is just a great, big rock. It gives off no light of its own. What we call moonlight is sunlight reflecting off the moon's light-gray surface. If you were standing on the moon, you would see light reflecting off Earth the same way.

at left: **craters on Earth's moon**

A planet-sized moon

28. Jupiter has more natural satellites than anything in our solar system. For many years, the count stood at 16, but new technology helped us discover many others in recent years. The count is now at least 63! Four of Jupiter's moons *(seen below)* are larger than Earth's moon. The largest, called Ganymede, is the largest moon in our solar system. In fact, it is larger than the planet Mercury.

Jupiter and its four largest moons

Jupiter

Io

Europa

Ganymede

Callisto

Other Things Up There

Up, up, and away!

Planets and moons are not the only celestial (suh-LES-chul) bodies in the solar system. (*Celestial* means "of or up in space.") Here are a few other celestial bodies that you should know about:

29. asteroid: a small, rocky object that orbits the sun. Most asteroids are part of a "belt" that is in orbit between Mars and Jupiter. *(See the picture on pages 10-11.)*

30. comet: a small celestial body with a bright core, traveling around the sun in an irregular orbit. Seen from Earth, a comet seems to have a fuzzy head, and sometimes a long bright tail. The fuzzy head and tail are dust, burning gases, and other matter streaming off the comet as it streaks through space.

31. meteor: a streak of light that we see in the sky when an asteroid or other small celestial body burns up as it enters and passes through Earth's atmosphere. People sometimes call meteors *shooting stars* or *falling stars*, because that is what they look like, but they are not stars.

32. meteorite: part of a meteor that makes it to Earth's surface without completely burning up.

Halley's comet

33. Edmond Halley (1656-1742) was an English scientist who noticed something that no one else had. He studied historic records of 24 comets that had appeared since 1337. He noticed that some seemed very similar— and that there was a pattern to those appearances. Three of those 24 comets, he believed, were the same comet. He predicted that it would return in 1758. It did, and was named in his honor.

asteroid 243, known as Ida *(left)*, and the tiny moon that orbits it *(right)*

See ya in '62!

34. Halley's is not the only comet in a regular orbit, but it is the most famous. We see it from Earth every 76 years or so, when its orbit around the sun brings it close enough for us to see. The last Halley's Comet "visit" was in 1986. If you missed it, you will have to wait until 2062 for the next one.

Galactic Facts

Getting in shape

35. Galaxies come in three main types:

• A **spiral galaxy** is one that has long, curving "arms" of stars. Our home galaxy, the Milky Way, is a spiral galaxy made up of about a hundred billion stars.

• An **elliptical** *(ih-LIP-tih-kul)* **galaxy** is oval-shaped, with a very bright center. (*Elliptical* means "oval-shaped.") If our galaxy was elliptical, so many stars would be shining on our planet that it would be bright all day and night.

• An **irregular galaxy** has no definite shape. It is neither spiral nor elliptical.

Home base

36. If you think of the Milky Way as a huge, spinning pinwheel with long, curving arms, where are we? Our sun is on one of the outer arms.

Howdy, neighbor!

37. The Milky Way's closest neighbor is another spiral galaxy, called Andromeda *(an-DRAH-muh-duh)*. Bigger, brighter Andromeda has twice as many stars as the Milky Way. On a clear night in the Northern Hemisphere, it is possible—but not easy—to see Andromeda with the naked eye. It looks like a faint splash of light in the sky. (It will be more clear if you have binoculars or a telescope.)

two galaxies: spiral *(at right)* and elliptical *(below)*

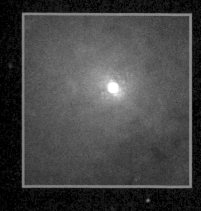

A long-distance call

38. A *light-year* is what it sounds like: the distance that light travels in a year. One light-year is 5.9 trillion miles. Yes, *trillion*! (One trillion is a 1 followed by 12 zeros.)

See the Light!

Closer than you think!

39. Our sun is much closer than a light-year. It is only eight light-minutes away. (Its light takes only eight minutes to reach Earth.) The next time you are watching a sunset, think of it this way: If it is 7:20 p.m. when you see the sun drop below the horizon, the light you are looking at left the sun at 7:12 p.m.

How far is far?

40. After our sun, the star closest to our planet is Proxima Centauri. Its light takes nearly 5.5 light-years to reach Earth.

41. Our sun is about 28,000 light-years from the Milky Way's center.

42. The Milky Way galaxy is about 100,000 light-years across

43. The Andromeda galaxy is about 2,000,000 light-years distant from the Milky Way.

at left: **our neighbor, the Andromeda galaxy (10 separate images put together to show the whole)**

part of the M16-Eagle Nebula, photographed by the Hubble Space Telescope in 1995

It's a Star's Life

44. A star has a life cycle. It is born, goes through several life stages, then dies.

45. First, there is a **nebula** *(NEB-yoo-luh).* (More than one are called nebulae—*NEB-yoo-lee.*) This is a huge, floating cloud of dust and gas—a star's basic ingredients.

46. Gravity makes a nebula collapse, forming a **protostar.** The gas and dust become so dense, hardly any light can pass through. The protostar continues to collapse, collecting more dust. It gets more and more dense, and hotter and hotter.

47. In time, the protostar's core reaches 15 million degrees. A protostar burns hydrogen and creates helium. (Both gases are found on Earth, too.) At this point, the burning ball of gas becomes a regular **star.**

48. After several billion years, the hydrogen starts to run out and the star begins to cool. It shines more brightly, and spreads outward. This is called a **red giant.** (Our sun will become a red giant in about five billion years. When it does, Mercury, Venus, and Earth will be destroyed.)

49. As a red giant expands, its outer layers of gas and dust break away and form new nebulae. All that is left of the star is its very small, very hot core. This is called a **white dwarf.**

50. As a small or medium-size star cools, it becomes a **yellow dwarf,** then a **red dwarf,** then a **brown dwarf** as its light slowly fades.

51. A bigger star ends in a huge explosion called a **supernova.** A supernova burns several billion times as bright as the star did. For a few days, it can burn brighter than an entire galaxy! After a supernova, the only thing left is either a black hole or a neutron *(NEW-tron)* star.

Who turned out the lights?

52. When a really huge star collapses, all that is left is a **black hole.** A black hole's force of gravity is so immense that everything nearby is sucked into it—even light.

Seeing the light

53. A **neutron star** is so densely packed that if you could scoop up a spoonful of its matter and take that back to Earth, that single spoonful would weigh about a billion tons!

54. A neutron star has two magnetic poles. (So does Earth.) As it spins, this star produces a bright beam of light from each pole. This makes the star seem to pulse: go bright, then dark, then bright. That is why spinning neutron stars are called **pulsars** *(PUHL-sarz).*

the Mz3-Ant Nebula, photographed by the Hubble Space Telescope in 1997-1998

Glow, baby, glow!

55. Binary stars are two stars that are kept close together by their gravity. From Earth, they can look like a single star going dark, then again. That is because, as they rotate, one sometimes blocks the other's light from our view, making it seem to go dark.

56. A **quasar** *(KWAY-zar)* is an object in space that gives off an intense light—brighter than 100 galaxies. Quasars are very old, and farther from us than anything else in the universe. A scientist studying them now is looking at light that is billions of years old!

The big bang

57. For hundreds, even thousands, of years, scientists have tried to figure out how the universe began. One idea is that 15 billion years

at right: a supernova photographed in 1987
above: the star it used to be, photographed in 1984

ago, a hot ball of matter exploded, creating gravity and electricity and thick clumps of particles. Over time, that stuff turned into atoms. *Atoms* are the tiny building blocks of everything in the universe, including the human body. Eventually, these atoms formed into stars. This idea is known as the **big bang theory.**

Hot argument

58. People have never agreed on how the universe—or even just our planet—was created. Some people believe the big-bang theory, but it is very complicated and hard to understand. Some people believe that the universe was created by an all-powerful god, Supreme Being, or higher form of intelligence. Some people have still other ideas. Nobody was there, so there is no record of what really happened.

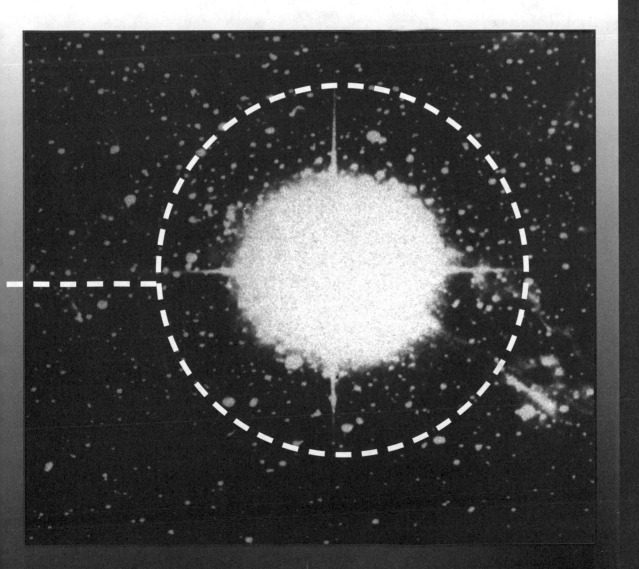

Eyes in the Skies

Satellites in the sky

59. A *satellite* is anything that orbits a planet. A satellite can be natural, such as a moon, or artificial (made by humans), such as a weather satellite.

the Hubble Space Telescope, high above Earth

Satellites and you

60. You may not realize it, but you probably use artificial satellites every day. If you make cell-phone calls, watch television, or listen to the radio, there is a good chance that a satellite is being used somewhere along the way. Meteorologists (scientists who study the weather) use satellite images to help them forecast the weather. Militaries and governments use satellite photos to spy on other countries. Satellites are used in countless other ways, too.

61. Have you ever heard of GPS—the global positioning system? Ship and plane pilots have used it for years. Now some cars have it. GPS uses signals that bounce off satellites in space to fix a location. It can "see" where you are, and tell you how to get where you want to go.

Farther than ever before

62. In 1990, NASA launched the Hubble Space Telescope (HST). Orbiting Earth from 375 miles above, it records space images around the clock and beams them back to astronomers on Earth.

63. Being so high lets the Hubble "see" much farther than any telescope on Earth. It has taken some amazing photographs. The space telescope was named for Edwin Powell Hubble (1889-1953), the scientist who discovered that other galaxies exist beyond the Milky Way. He also discovered that the universe is expanding—and has been, very slowly, over billions of years.

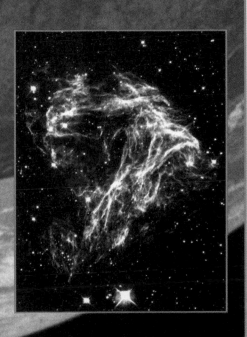

three images taken by the HST: the Pistol Nebula with a huge star (top); Mars (center); and debris left over from an exploding star (bottom)

Studying Our Neighbors

What do we know about our neighbors in our solar system? Quite a lot, thanks to some very special helpers—space probes. A *probe* is a device designed to go where humans can't. Probes send back pictures and other kinds of information for scientists to study.

the *Galileo* space probe

Double whammies

64. In 1975 and 1976, NASA sent probes to Mars, our nearest outside neighbor. The probes, called *Viking 1* and *Viking 2*, sent back a lot of information on "the Red Planet." Like many space probes, each *Viking* craft had two parts, an orbiter and a lander. (An *orbiter* circles the planet, sending back sky-high views and data on the planet's atmosphere. A *lander* explores the planet's surface.) The information sent back led scientists to believe that Mars once had water on its surface.

65. During the winter of 2003-2004, NASA landed two more probes on Mars. *Opportunity* and *Spirit* beamed back the clearest-ever images of the Martian landscape—picture-perfect views from 64 million miles away.

A long, long way to go

66. A space probe called *Galileo*, launched in October 1989, did not reach Jupiter until December 1995! The orbiter made 34 trips around the huge planet before being crushed by Jupiter's dense atmosphere in September 2003. The information that *Galileo* sent back will keep scientists busy for years to come. (*Galileo* took the asteroid photo on pages 14-15.)

Well-named craft

67. *Voyager 1* and *Voyager 2* have traveled far beyond any human-made craft ever. *Voyager 1* visited Jupiter and Saturn. *Voyager 2* visited Jupiter, Saturn, Uranus, and Neptune! Launched in 1977, they are still out there, sending us data from deep space. (One of the *Voyager* probes took the five photos that were joined to create the scene on page 13.)

a painting showing *Galileo*'s 1995 arrival at Jupiter

Looking for Life

E.T., where are you?

68. Scientists plan to continue using probes to search for signs of extraterrestrial life. (The word *extraterrestrial* describes anything that is outside Earth and its atmosphere.) Among the many people and groups carrying on the search is an organization called the SETI Institute. (*SETI* is short for Search for Extraterrestrial Intelligence.) SETI employs 130 people whose full-time mission is to search for life beyond Earth. They may not find a being like E.T., the hero of Steven Spielberg's famous movie, but they do hope to find some sign that our planet is not the only one to have life.

Dr. Carl Sagan, a famous astronomer, led a team of people who decided what to put on the *Voyager* Golden Records. Here, he is standing with a model of *Voyager 2*.

69. If a *Voyager* probe is ever discovered by extraterrestrial beings, will they know where it came from? To help, NASA scientists attached a "Golden Record" to each *Voyager* spacecraft. The 12-inch copper disks carry sounds and pictures that represent life on Earth. Among more than 100 things recorded on the disks are the sounds of waves splashing on a beach, music, and people speaking 55 different languages. There also is a written message, from U.S. President Jimmy Carter, and a set of picture instructions on how to play the disk.

at right: instructions on a Golden Record cover

above: preparing a Golden Record

attaching disk to *Voyager 1*

Getting There

A real rocket scientist

70. Much of what we first knew about rocket science came from Robert H. Goddard. Often called the "Father of Modern Rocketry," Goddard (1882-1945) perfected the use of liquid fuel for rocket engines. The same basic technique is used in rocket engines today. On March 16, 1926, Goddard set off his first successful rocket. It shot 41 feet high and 184 feet away in just 2.5 seconds. In 1935, he shot a liquid-fuel rocket faster than the speed of sound—another first. Within just a few decades, rockets much like Goddard's were carrying humans into outer space.

launch of one of NASA's space shuttles (in use since 1981)

Robert H. Goddard, with the first-ever liquid-fuel rocket (1926)

launch of the *Apollo 11* spacecraft (1969)

Rockets went from this . . . *to this*

external tank

solid rocket boosters

orbiter

. . . to this!

Blastoff!

71. Take a look at this photo. For takeoff, an **orbiter** (space shuttle) is attached to a large **external tank** (ET) that has two **solid rocket boosters** (SRBs). The SRBs provide most of the thrust (force) needed to lift everything off the launching pad. The orbiter's three engines also provide some thrust.

72. After two minutes, the SRBs stop burning. They drop away and fall 28 miles back to Earth. Parachutes help them drop safely into the Atlantic Ocean, where shipboard NASA workers retrieve them. (SRBs can be used again.)

73. The external tank holds liquid hydrogen, which fuels the orbiter's engines, and liquid oxygen. About eight and a half minutes after takeoff, the shuttle reaches orbit and its main engines cut off. When that happens, the ET drops off. Unlike the SRBs, it doesn't fall into the ocean. It breaks apart and burns up in Earth's atmosphere.

74. To resist the pull of gravity and stay in space, a space shuttle has to travel at 18,000 miles per hour. If a car moved that fast, you could drive from New York City to Hollywood, California, in 10 minutes! (In a regular car, that trip would take 42 hours—if you drove straight across, nonstop.)

First up

75. From the 1950s through the 1980s, the U.S. and Soviet Union were in a "space race." The two countries worked hard to be the first to send objects and people into space. The Soviets scored the first big move on October 4, 1957. That is when they sent the first man-made satellite into space. *Sputnik 1 (below),* which weighed 184.3 pounds, went as high as 584 miles above Earth and stayed in orbit for several months.

Laika, the first Earthling in space

Sputnik 1

It's a bird!
It's a plane!
It's a—dog?

76. The Soviets also sent the first living beings into space orbit. The first was a dog named Laika *(LYE-kuh),* sent up in *Sputnik 2* on November 3, 1957. Back then, scientists knew little about the dangers of space travel. Instead of rocketing people into space, they sent animals. (The first animal sent into space by Americans was a chimpanzee named Ham, sent up on January 31, 1961.) All of the animals returned to Earth safely.

Where no man had gone before

77. The first human being to travel in space was a Soviet cosmonaut named Yuri A. Gagarin *(guh-GAR-un)*. On April 12, 1961, Gagarin was launched into space aboard a spacecraft called *Vostok 1*. Traveling as high as 187 miles above Earth, Gagarin's craft made one orbit of Earth, then landed back in the Soviet Union. The whole trip took just 1 hour and 48 minutes. Gagarin's amazing feat won him worldwide fame.

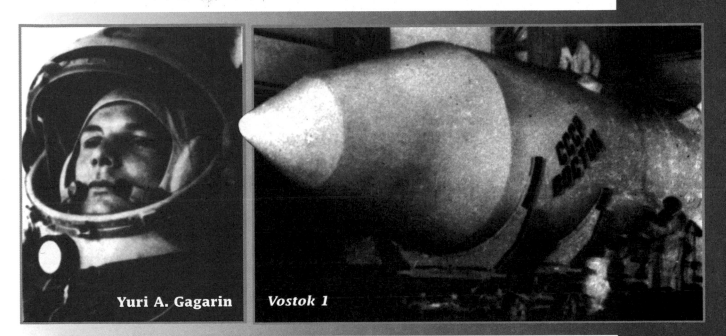

Yuri A. Gagarin   *Vostok 1*

Valentina Tereshkova

Where no woman had gone before

78. The first woman in space was another Soviet cosmonaut, Valentina Tereshkova *(ter-ush-KOH-vuh)*. Launched aboard *Vostok 6* on June 16, 1963, she made 48 Earth orbits in 71 hours, then landed safely. The second woman in space was another Soviet, Svetlana Savitskaya, who made her first space flight in 1982.

Space Race, Part 2
The Americans

NASA jumps in

79. In 1958, the U.S. government created NASA—the National Aeronautics and Space Administration. NASA handles all space-related activities for the United States. Its staff worked hard to catch up with the Soviets in the space race. That did not take long. The first U.S. satellite in space, *Explorer 1*, was launched on January 31, 1958. In 1961, NASA launched its Mercury program, aimed at getting humans into space.

Ham the space chimp

the original Mercury astronauts—*top row (left to right):* **Alan B. Shepard Jr., Virgil I. (Gus) Grissom, and L. Gordon Cooper Jr.;** *bottom row (left to right):* **Walter Schirra Jr., Donald K. (Deke) Slayton, John H. Glenn Jr., and M. Scott Carpenter**

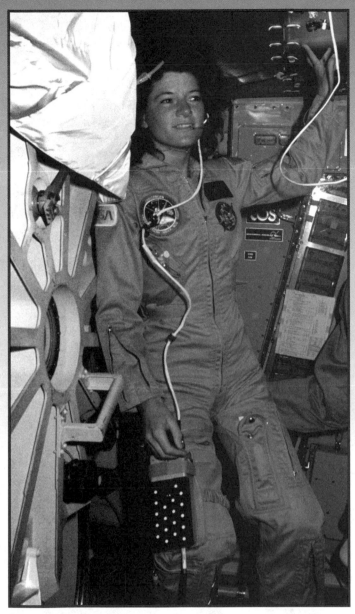

Sally Ride, floating weightless in space

American pioneers

80. The first American in space was Alan B. Shepard Jr. On May 5, 1961—just 23 days after Gagarin's flight—Shepard rocketed into space aboard the *Freedom 7*. He rose 115 miles above Earth before coming back down, safely splashing into the Atlantic Ocean.

81. On July 21, 1961, Virgil I. (Gus) Grissom made a flight similar to Shepard's, becoming the third person and second American in space. In March 1963, Grissom became the first person to go into space a second time. On that flight, he controlled his spacecraft while inside it—another first. (Before then, spacecraft were run by remote control, from command centers on Earth.)

82. John H. Glenn Jr. was the first American to orbit Earth. His *Friendship 7* space capsule blasted off on February 20, 1962. In 4 hours, 55 minutes, and 23 seconds, Glenn made 3 orbits—traveling 75,679 miles at a speed of about 17,500 miles per hour! Glenn became a U.S. senator in 1974, but made space history again in 1998. At age 77, he served as a crew member aboard the space shuttle *Discovery*, becoming the oldest person to travel in space.

83. The first American woman in space was Sally K. Ride. She served as mission specialist on the space shuttle *Challenger* in June 1983, and returned to space in October 1984. On both missions, she launched satellites and ran scientific experiments.

Going Lunar

An impossible dream?

84. On May 25, 1961, U.S. President John F. Kennedy made a speech. In it, he called for the U.S. to put a man on the moon before the end of the decade. At the time, that seemed like a next-to-impossible task. But on July 20, 1969, it happened: Neil Armstrong, a NASA astronaut, became the first person to set foot on the moon.

Amazing success

85. NASA's moon landing program was called Apollo. A number of Apollo test flights went up before Apollo 11, launched on July 16, 1969. Inside were astronauts Neil Armstrong, Edwin (Buzz) Aldrin, and Michael Collins. Their *Saturn V* spacecraft was in two parts. When they reached the moon, the two parts split. A **command module** called *Columbia* stayed in orbit. A small **lunar module** called *Eagle* landed on the moon. On July 20, at 10:56 p.m. Eastern Time, Armstrong took his first step onto the moon's surface and spoke these now-famous words: "This is one small step for man, one giant leap for mankind."

86. Armstrong and Aldrin spent 21 hours on the moon. They planted a U.S. flag and collected moon rocks for scientists to study. (Collins remained aboard the *Columbia*.) Then the *Eagle* rose, reconnected with the *Columbia*, and all three astronauts returned safely to Earth.

> *"I believe that this nation should commit itself to achieving the goal, before this decade is out, of landing a man on the moon and returning him safely to the Earth."*
> —President John F. Kennedy
> May 25, 1961

87. Only 12 people (so far!) have ever set foot on the moon. In all, NASA made six successful moon landings. The last two people to walk on the moon were Apollo 17's Eugene A. Cernan and Harrison H. Schmitt, in December 1972.

Going for zero

88. A space shuttle flying at 18,000 miles per hour creates a force strong enough to balance out gravity. When this force—called centrifugal *(sen-TRIF-yoo-gul)* force—is equal with gravity, people and things become weightless, and float in space. This is called zero gravity.

Fly-by training

89. To get used to the feeling of zero gravity, astronauts-in-training ride inside a hollowed-out jet plane. The plane is attached to something that makes it swoop up and down like a giant roller coaster. At the top of each loop, anyone inside the plane is weightless for about 30 seconds. Astronaut Barbara Morgan remembers the thrill of feeling weightless for the first time. "I just shot to the ceiling," she says. "I just burst out laughing!"

food prepared for *Skylab* astronauts

astronauts-in-training, getting used to zero gravity

Barbara Morgan

It isn't as easy as it looks!

90. Zero gravity presents special challenges for people out in space. For instance:

● Astronauts use their hands to help them move from place to place, because their feet will not stay on the ground.

● Astronauts would float up off any mattress, so they sleep inside zipped-up hammocks.

● Instead of taking showers, astronauts get clean by using washcloths, which soak up the water and soap.

● Astronauts squeeze their drinks out of bags directly into their mouths. Liquid will float out of a cup. (For fun, astronauts sometimes squeeze orange juice into the air and watch it float around in tiny globs.)

● Space food is made so that it sticks together. Zero gravity makes any other kind of food—candy pieces, for instance—very tricky to eat. "M&Ms are a real mess!" says astronaut Jeff Ashby. He remembers when one of his crewmates on the space shuttle *Atlantis* opened a bag and tried to catch the small candies in her mouth. It didn't work. "They go every which way," says Ashby.

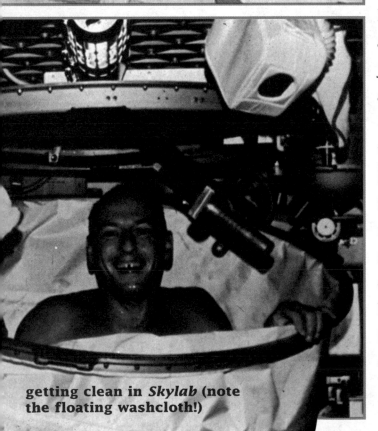

getting clean in *Skylab* (note the floating washcloth!)

astronauts Carl J. Meade *(left)* and Mark C. Lee, testing safety equipment in space (Lee is tethered to the shuttle, Meade isn't!)

Let's Take a Walk!

91. Imagine stepping outside of a spacecraft while you are hundreds of miles above Earth! That is a space walk, which NASA calls an EVA—extravehicular activity. (*Extravehicular* means "outside the vehicle.") In zero gravity, an EVA is more of a float than a walk.

92. The first person to ever walk in space was Alexei Leonov, a Soviet cosmonaut, on March 18, 1965. Soon after that, on June 3, Ed White became the first American to do it. Since then, space walks have become common. Astronauts perform them to repair spacecraft and satellites, build space stations, and conduct experiments.

93. Walking in space may sound like fun and look easy, but it is dangerous and difficult. Astronauts wear special suits that keep air pressure and oxygen at safe levels. To keep from flying off in zero gravity, they must move slowly and carefully. For safety, astronauts are usually tied down. So are any tools and equipment they use.

94. To train for EVAs, astronauts wearing space suits are lowered to the bottom of a 40-foot-deep pool. There, they practice working on replicas of the space shuttle and space station. They also use virtual reality, wearing a helmet with goggles that gives them a computer-generated view of the station.

The large object in the background of all three of these photos is planet Earth.

Mark C. Lee in 1994, space walking above the space shuttle *Discovery*

Ed White during his 1965 space walk

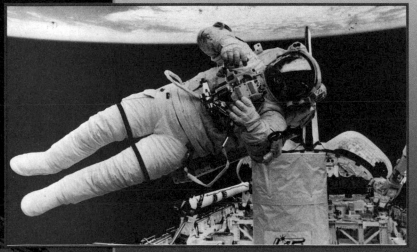

A Base in Space

95. A *space station* is a craft built to stay in orbit for a period of time, to serve as a base for people living and working in space. The world's first-ever space station was *Salyut 1,* launched into space by the Soviet Union on April 19, 1971. The first working U.S. space station was *Skylab,* launched on May 14, 1973.

96. Between 1974 and 2000, six other space stations were used for various periods of time, then shut down: the Soviet Union's *Salyuts 3, 4, 5, 6,* and *7,* and Russia's *Mir (meer).*

mission specialist John B. Herrington *(far left),* working on a section of the International Space Station connected to the space shuttle *Endeavor*

photo of a section of the ISS in 2001, just after being disconnected from space shuttle *Discovery*

A city in the stars

98. When the ISS is complete, scientists, doctors, and experts in other fields will go there to study space, stars, and the planets as no one has ever done before. Researchers hope to make advances in space travel, manufacturing, medicine, and technology.

shuttle commander Jeff Ashby, suiting up for a mission to construct the ISS

This is ISS!

97. The world's ninth space station—the International Space Station (ISS)—is under construction. Sixteen countries, including the U.S., are involved in building it. Some other facts about the ISS:

• The first two pieces of it were launched into place in 1998.

• The cost of building it is $60 billion.

• It is about the size of two football fields: 360 feet across, 290 feet long.

• Traveling at 17,500 miles per hour, it makes one complete Earth orbit every 90 minutes.

• Its altitude is 250 miles above Earth.

• Much of its construction is done by space-walking astronauts.

• When completed (in April 2006), it will weigh one million pounds.

Is Space in Your Future?

Home, sweet home?

99. Colonies in space are popular settings for sci-fi stories. These are places where ordinary humans—not just astronauts—live and work. Might they be real someday? Many people think so, including NASA researchers. They picture huge settlements in orbit around Earth. Each colony would hold everything necessary for life: air, water, crops, and so on. It would rotate, as Earth does, to create its own gravity inside, allowing people to move about the same way they do on Earth.

an artist's idea of a space colony, in a cutaway view showing the inside as well as the outside

What would you like?

100. Why live in space? Different people have different ideas. Space colonies could provide plenty of land, if Earth's human population outgrows our space. They could serve as scientific research stations, as the International Space Station does now. They could provide environments created for people with special needs, such as lower gravity to help disabled people move freely. They could be safe places for prisons, keeping criminals a safe distance away. What would *you* use it for?

The Last Word

101. Could outer space be your next home? Probably not, but perhaps it will be your children's. After all, as the space settlements page on NASA's Web site points out, "A hundred years ago, nobody had ever flown in an airplane, but today nearly 500 million people a year fly."

Space Quiz:
Can you soar among the stars?

1. **The sun's heat comes from which of the following?**
   a. fire
   b. melting wax
   c. nuclear reactions
   d. water

2. **Who first claimed that everything revolves around the sun?**
   a. Nicolaus Copernicus
   b. Galileo Galilei
   c. John Glenn
   d. Carl Sagan

3. **The huge explosion that ends a star's life is called what?**
   a. pulsar
   b. red giant
   c. supernova
   d. white dwarf

4. **Which of these is *not* a type of galaxy?**
   a. elliptical
   b. irregular
   c. spherical
   d. spiral

5. **How long does light from the sun take to reach Earth?**
   a. 8 minutes
   b. 64 minutes
   c. 10 hours
   d. 3 days

6. **Which of these planets is *not* made out of rock?**
   a. Jupiter
   b. Mars
   c. Mercury
   d. Pluto

7. **A black hole is created when a huge star does what?**
   a. crashes into another star
   b. collapses
   c. goes into orbit
   d. is born

8. **Space probes called *Opportunity* and *Spirit* landed where?**
   a. on Mars
   b. on Mercury
   c. on Saturn
   d. on Venus

9. **In 1957, the Soviet Union had the first victory in the space race with the United States by doing what?**
   a. building a space station
   b. launching a man-made satellite
   c. sending a man to the moon
   d. visiting Mars

10. **The SETI Institute is an organization that does what?**
    a. builds space shuttles for NASA
    b. operates space colonies
    c. searches for life beyond Earth
    d. trains astronauts for space walks

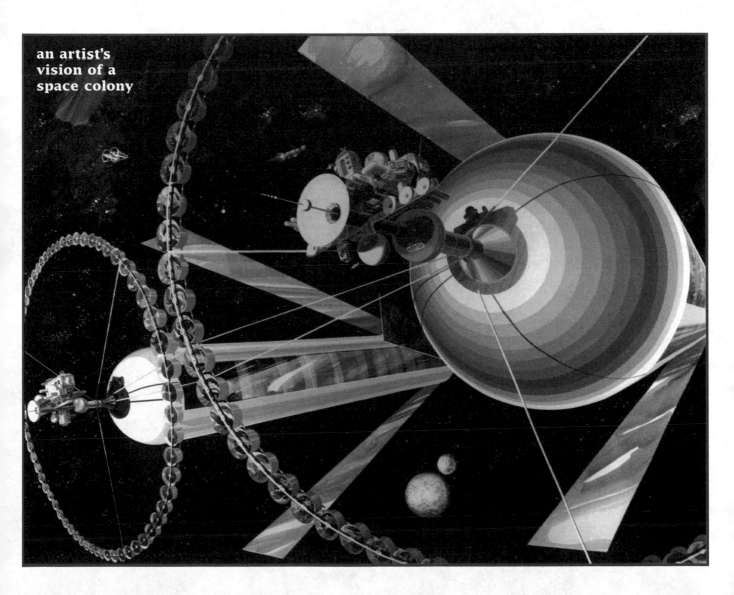

an artist's vision of a space colony

Buzz Aldrin on the moon (reflected in his visor are the lunar module and Neil Armstrong, taking the picture)